P9-ECI-864

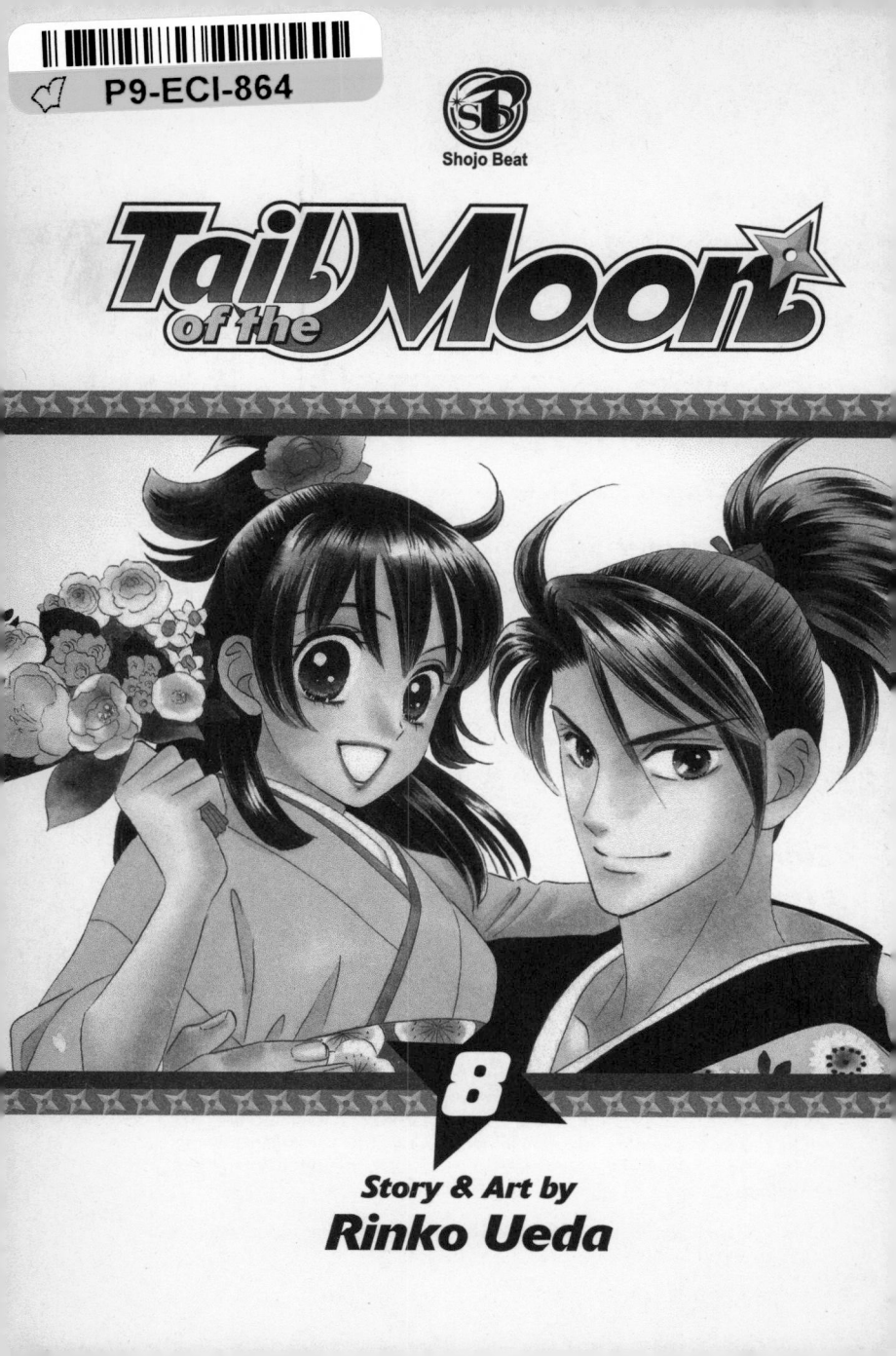

# Tail of the Moon

## Volume 8

CONTENTS


Chapter 50 ..... 4

Chapter 51 ..... 33

Chapter 52 ..... 59

Chapter 53 ..... 85

Chapter 54 ..... 111

Chapter 55 ..... 137

Chapter 56 ..... 163

Glossary ..... 188


## Story Thus Far...

It is the Era of the Warring States. Usagi is a failure as a ninja, but she is a skilled herbalist. She is working hard to qualify as a ninja so she can be the bride of Hattori Hanzo (aka "Shimo no Hanzo")!

Usagi sets out to Azuchi to meet Oda Nobunaga. Hanzo accompanies her in disguise as her husband Hanbei, a samurai from Okazaki. On the way, the two share their feelings and finally feel connected to one another.

As it turns out, Usagi does not get to meet Nobunaga after all. However, she does remember seeing Nobunaga's page, Ranmaru, back in Kouga. Unfortunately, Ranmaru discovers that Usagi is wearing a wig! Usagi is worried that Ranmaru will remember her as a ninja, but he does not seem to notice. Afraid that her engagement to Hanzo will become null again due to her incompetence, Usagi decides to keep this matter a secret from Hanzo.

Just when Usagi and Hanzo decide to go back to Iga, Ranmaru suddenly says, "I'll accompany you to Okazaki"...!

I'LL BE ACCOMPANYING YOU TO OKAZAKI.
OH, NO...!

Chapter 50
Tail of the Moon

TAIL OF THE MOON EXTRA: TODAY'S MISSION

"I WANT TO SEE HANZO DOING MATSUKEN SAMBA!"

-ABARENBO SHOGUN, TOKYO

SORRY TO KEEP YOU WAITING.
WELL THEN...
...LET'S HEAD OUT FOR OKAZAKI.
MOSUKE, LET ME GO...
KEEEE...
MOSUKE...
WHAT ARE WE GOING TO DO?!
THE GUYS BACK AT OKAZAKI DON'T KNOW ANYTHING ABOUT THIS!
HMM...

TROMP
TROMP
OH!
RANMARU...
HANZOU WOULD LIKE TO BORROW A HORSE SO THAT HE CAN RETURN TO OKAZAKI FIRST.
DON'T PULL MY HAIR...!!
KEE...!
CLOP
CLOP
CLOP
I HAVE TO TELL EVERYBODY AT OKAZAKI ABOUT THIS...
...OR IT'LL CAUSE PROBLEMS FOR LORD IEYASU AS WELL.

USAGI, PLEASE COME BACK AGAIN TO SEE MOSUKE.
KEE...
KEE...
MOSUKE, PLEASE CALM DOWN...
SURE...
I LIKE MOSUKE, BUT I DON'T WANT TO COME BACK TO AZUCHI...
IF ONLY THINGS WERE DIFFERENT...
SIGH...
I WOULD HAVE GONE STRAIGHT BACK TO IGA...
...AND MARRIED HANZO...
WHAT??
TWITCH
BRUSH
YOUR HAIR WAS TANGLED UP, SO I...

GRIN
RANMARU...
IF I TOLD YOU, IT WOULDN'T BE A SECRET ANYMORE, NOW WOULD IT?

IT'S OKAY, I'LL DO IT MYSELF.
WSP
WSP
BUT IT'S SUPPOSED TO BE A SECRET, RIGHT?
WHAT'S A SECRET?

RAN-MARU...
DON'T MESS AROUND WITH A GROWN-UP LIKE ME.
AAAARGH... HANZO'S REALLY FROWNING...
It's scary...

HANZO'S IN A BAD MOOD...
...BECAUSE HE'S JEALOUS?

TROMP
OF COURSE.
TROMP

AH, THAT'S RIGHT.
JEALOUSY IS A CHILDISH EMOTION FOR A GROWN-UP LIKE YOU.
NOW WHAT'S HE SAYING...?

WATCH YOUR STEP AS YOU GO DOWN.
USAGI.
BUT THAT'S ...
...BECAUSE HE CARES FOR ME, RIGHT? ♡
HUH?!
USA...
HEE... ♡

USA...!
SPRUNG
MAMEZO!
HUG
I'VE FOUND YOU AT LAST...!
!!

MAMEZO IS OUR CHILD.
HUH?
WH...WHO IS THIS BOY...?
THE PIGLET?!
USA...
THE PIGLET'S DIS-APPEARED...
MAMEZO...
MOUTHS WORDS
DON'T LET HIM FIND OUT THAT YOU'RE A NINJA!
DI...DID HE JUST JUMP OFF THAT ROOF...?!
NOW, MAMEZO...
STRAIGHTEN YOURSELF OUT AND SAY HELLO TO RANMARU.
HE'S A VERY ACTIVE BOY...
PLEASE...
PLEASE KNOW HOW TO LIP-READ!
IF HE FINDS OUT THAT YOU'RE A NINJA, WE'LL ALL BE KILLED!!
MOUTHS WORDS
STARE

GLOWER
FIDGET
FIDGET
M...
...MY...
SNIFF
...NAME IS...
...MAMEZO...
SAY HELLO TO HIM.
BUT HOW DID A CHILD LIKE HIM GET THROUGH THE MAIN GATE...?
HE'S SMALL, SO HE MUST HAVE SLIPPED THROUGH.
HUG
WHEN DID YOU GIVE BIRTH TO HIM, USAGI?!
UM...
WAAAARGH!
WELL DONE.
I'M PROUD OF YOU, MAMEZO!!
MY FIRST WIFE DIED RIGHT AFTER SHE GAVE BIRTH TO HIM...
HE'S A CHILD FROM MY PREVIOUS MARRIAGE.
WHA-

# GREETINGS

Hello, it's Ue-Rin.

"Ue-Rin's Manga School" is gradually getting to the most interesting part...

My glasses...

My glasses...

I keep misplacing my glasses these days...

The story continues from the summer of my third year in middle school when I went down to Osaka to meet the editor with my two pieces of manga...

I'LL SEE YOU LATER THEN...
VERY WELL.
I'LL BRING ALL YOUR DINNERS TO THIS ROOM.
EXHAUSTED...
USA, HANG IN THERE...
INN SUZUYA
OHH-KAY.
I'm sure the piglet's got its reasons...
What reasons ...?
BY THE WAY, USAGI...
DON'T RAISE YOUR VOICES.
SHHHK
HUSH
YOU MUSTN'T LOWER YOUR GUARD UNTIL THE ASSIGNMENT IS FINISHED.
BUT MY PIGLET...
AW, JEEZ...
WHY DID YOU HAVE TO SHOW UP SO SUDDENLY, MAMEZO?

WHAT IS THIS SECRET THAT RANMARU WAS TALKING ABOUT?
TALK ABOUT GETTING TO THE POINT!
UM...RA... RANMARU...
...ASKED ME ABOUT HOW HANBEI AND I MET AND GOT MARRIED, SO I JUST GAVE HIM A RANDOM ANSWER...
I ALSO TOLD HIM, "DON'T TELL HANBEI THAT I TOLD YOU ABOUT IT"...
THAT'S ALL...
IS THAT REALLY ALL THERE IS TO IT?
RE... REALLY.
THIS IS HURTING MY HEART...
THROB
THROB
THEN THAT'S FINE.
BUT, USAGI...

OHH...
THROB
PLEASE DON'T HIDE ANYTHING FROM ME.
I'M SO SORRY, HANZO!!
SNIFF
FORGIVE ME FOR LYING TO YOU...!
USA, ARE YOU CRYING?
MAMEZO...
YOU MUST PRACTICE CALLING ME "FATHER."
SNIFF
THE SECRET RANMARU WAS REFERRING TO...
D...
...DADDY?
B-BUMP
B-BUMP
NOT "DADDY"...
..."FATHER."
...IS ABOUT MY WIG...

USAGI...
AREN'T YOU HUNGRY?
I'M TOO TIRED...
THAT'S NOT GOOD.
I'VE GOT SOME MEDICINE, SO WHY DON'T YOU TAKE SOME?
NAH...
IT'S NOT THAT BAD...
FATHER...
WHAT'S THIS?
THAT'S A TYPE OF FISH CALLED "EEL."
Sigh...
BUT I CAN'T TELL YOU THAT I SAW RANMARU IN KOUGA!
I'M REALLY REALLY SORRY...!!

WHAT'S THE MATTER?
...NOTHING!
ER...
WHISPER
PLEASE DROP BY MY ROOM LATER.
HUH?
MAMEZO, THIS EEL'S DELICIOUS, ISN'T IT?
UH-HUH! ♡
DROP BY HIS ROOM...?
I DON'T WANT TO KEEP ANY MORE SECRETS FROM HANZO...
OOH, THIS IS SO GOOD...

USAGI, DON'T LEAVE THIS ROOM UNTIL WE COME BACK.
SEE YOU LATER...
HUH?
WHY?!
PHEW

MAMEZO.
LET'S GO AND TAKE A BATH.
YES, FATHER.

DON'T TALK TO HIM UNLESS IT IS ABSOLUTELY NECESSARY!!
Keep your wig on.
KPK
Ow!
RANMARU IS A DANGEROUS PERSON.

SNEAK

I FEEL LIKE I'M DOING SOMETHING REALLY BAD...
IT...
...IT'S ME, USAGI...
SNEAK
SNEAK

I CAN'T...
I'M SORRY, HANZO...

OKAY...
UNDER-STAND?
I WANT TO FOLLOW YOUR ORDERS, BUT...

ZIIK
I'VE BEEN WAITING FOR YOU.
PLEASE COME IN...
WHATEVER I'M HERE FOR, LET'S TAKE CARE OF IT OUT HERE!
WHAT...
I...I'M HANBEI'S WIFE...
...SO I CAN'T ENTER A MAN'S ROOM AT NIGHT!!
USAGI...
YOU REALLY LOVE HANBEI FROM THE BOTTOM OF YOUR HEART, DON'T YOU?
LOVE?!

...A STRONGER FEELING THAN "LIKE," ISN'T IT?
LOVE'S...
TH-THUMP TH-THUMP
PLEASE WAIT HERE THEN.
I GUESS... I TRULY DO LOVE HIM, DON'T I?
HERE YOU ARE, USAGI.
THIS IS A WESTERN SWEET CALLED CASTELLA.
SWEET THINGS ARE GOOD FOR YOUR BODY WHEN YOU'RE TIRED.
UM...
...IS THAT ALL?
I'VE ONLY GOT ONE, SO DON'T TELL THE OTHERS ABOUT IT.
OH, NO...
...THAT'S NOT WHAT I MEANT...
WELL, THAT'S ALL.
GOOD NIGHT.
SHHHK
...
THIS WAS WHY HE TOLD ME TO COME?!

ZWAK
GULP!
IT'S JUST CAKE.
OH WELL.
It'll be gone once I eat it...
NOW I'VE GOT ANOTHER SECRET TO HIDE FROM HANZO...
USA, DO YOU WANT SOME WATER?!
WHAT'S WRONG?!
COUGH!
THUMP THUMP
MY...
...MY THROA...
IT'S NOTHING SPECIAL.
WHAT KIND OF SWEET?
JU... JUST A SWEET...
WHAT WERE YOU EATING BEHIND MY BACK?
CHUG CHUG

WHAT...
YOU BROKE YOUR PROMISE...
YOU MET WITH RANMARU, DIDN'T YOU?
I THOUGHT I TOLD YOU NOT TO HIDE ANYTHING FROM ME!

REALLY!
HE JUST GAVE ME A SWEET, THAT'S ALL...
IS THAT REALLY ALL?!
YOU THINK THERE'S SOMETHING BETWEEN ME AND RANMARU...?!
...
WHY?

THE ONE THAT I LIKE IS YOU, HANZO.
I'VE ALWAYS TOLD YOU HOW I FELT.
WHY WON'T YOU BELIEVE ME?
I'VE ALWAYS...
...LOVED YOU, HANZO...
SILENCE!

HUH...

WHISPER
DON'T FORGET THAT.
I'M HANBEI RIGHT NOW.
I'M SORRY I DOUBTED YOU...

HANZO'S BREATH FEELS SO HOT...
FROM THE FIRST TIME I MET YOU...
...I KNEW THAT YOU WERE HEAD OVER HEELS IN LOVE WITH ME.

MY BODY FEELS LIKE IT'S GOING TO MELT AWAY...

## TAIL OF THE MOON EXTRA: TODAY'S MISSION

"I WANT TO SEE HANZO AND BENKEI TOGETHER!"

–RYOKO, KYOTO

THE SPANISH ANTHEM DOES NOT HAVE ANY LYRICS.
HANZO'S TRIVIA
Tail of the Moon
Chapter 51

MELT ME...
...SOME MORE...

VEEN
OH!
MA... MAMEZO!!
USA, I'M SO GLAD YOU GOT TO KISS HANZO...
UH-HUH !!
HANZO, LET'S CONTINUE... ♡
MMMM
YOU IDIOT.
NOT IN FRONT OF A CHILD...
WHOA.
USA, YOU'VE GOT A NOSE-BLEED!!
DRIBBLE...
HUH?

URGH...
PAT PAT
FOR GOD'S SAKE...
IF YOU KEEP ENDING UP LIKE THIS WITH JUST A KISS...
...YOU'RE NEVER GOING TO BE ABLE TO PERFORM ANY CONJUGAL ACTS.
WHAT'S A CONJUGAL ACT?
YOU DON'T NEED TO KNOW YET, MAMEZO.
!!

Get ready.
IT'S TIME TO CUDDLE TOGETHER.
USAGI...
A CONJUGAL ACT...!!
...IS SOMETHING EVEN MORE BREATH-TAKING THAN KISSING, ISN'T IT??
ZORT
!!
WAAARGH
DON'T STAIN THE ROOM!!
USA'S NOSEBLEED WON'T STOP...
ONCE WE GET BACK TO IGA AND GET MARRIED, THEN WE'LL... ♡

THAT'S MEDICINE ?!
YUP... IT'S THE ROOT OF THE PLANT RUBIA AKANE...
IF YOU BOIL IT IN WATER, THE RESULTING BREW HELPS RELIEVE ANEMIA.
SHOULD WE WALK SLOWER?
I...I'M FINE...
I'LL TAKE SOME MEDICINE...
TROMP
TROMP
USAGI...
...YOU DON'T LOOK WELL.
SLUMP
I'M JUST A LITTLE ANEMIC...
HOW DID YOU KNOW?!
NO... USAGI IS...
COULD IT BE THAT YOU GREW UP IN THE MOUNTAINS, USAGI?
YOU SEEM TO KNOW A LOT ABOUT HERBS.
I GUESS ANY MOUNTAIN VILLAGE IS PRETTY MUCH THE SAME...
WHAT KIND OF...?
WHAT KIND OF PLACE IS IT?
I... I GREW UP IN THE MOUNTAINS, BUT RIGHT BY OKAZAKI...
OH...
YOU IDIOT.

I'VE BEEN TO A LOT OF PLACES...
WELL, THERE ARE MOUNTAINS AS FAR AS THE EYE CAN SEE, AND THERE AREN'T ANY SHOPS AROUND OR ANYTHING...
...BUT IT'S A WONDERFUL PLACE WITH LOTS OF HERBS AND FRUITS.
...BUT I LIKE IGA THE MOST.
IT SOUNDS LIKE A GREAT PLACE.
RIGHT... ♬
YOU TOO, MAMEZO ?!
THERE'S LOTS OF PLACES TO PLAY TOO... ♪
THERE'S A LARGE WAR COMING SOON...
ALAS, I WON'T HAVE TIME TO DO THAT FOR A WHILE...
OH.
IS THAT SO?
PHEW
I'D LOVE TO SEE WHERE YOU GREW UP.
UH...
THAT WOULD BE A MAJOR PROBLEM...!!

WHAT DID HE JUST SAY?
WAR...?
THE ATTACK ON IGA.
I'M ON MY WAY TO OKAZAKI TO REQUEST LORD IEYASU'S COOPERATION WITH US FOR THE WAR...

NO...
AND WHEN IS THAT ATTACK GOING TO TAKE PLACE?
THE EXACT DATE HASN'T BEEN DECIDED YET, BUT...
...IT'LL PROBABLY OCCUR AROUND THE BEGINNING OF THE NEW YEAR...
THE BEGINNING OF THE NEW YEAR...
WE'VE GOT LESS THAN THREE MONTHS?!
A WAR!!
WAAARGH
I DON'T WANT A WAR...
IT'S NOTHING FOR YOU TO CRY ABOUT, MAMEZO.
I'M SORRY...
...FOR TALKING ABOUT IT IN FRONT OF YOUR CHILD...

IF HE FINDS OUT NOW, EVERYTHING WE'VE DONE WILL BE WASTED!!
THERE, THERE...
IT'S OKAY...
Sorry...
BUT DON'T WORRY...IT HAS NOTHING TO DO WITH OKAZAKI, WHERE YOU LIVE.
WAAARGH
MAMEZO...
COME HERE!
I MUSTN'T SEEM UPSET!!
WE'RE ALMOST AT OKAZAKI CASTLE.
I HAVE TO ACT CALM LIKE HANZO.
YOU MUST RETURN TO AZUCHI IMMEDIATELY!!
RANMARU!
CLOP
CLOP
CLOP

BEARDED HANZO!!
WHAT-EVER IS THE MATTER?
WE'VE RECEIVED INFORMATION THAT THERE IS GOING TO BE AN ASSASSINATION ATTEMPT ON LORD NOBUNAGA!!
WHAT?!
USE THIS HORSE TO RETURN TO AZUCHI!!
AN ASSAS-SINATION ATTEMPT ON NOBUNAGA ?!
VERY WELL.
PLEASE HAND LORD NOBUNAGA'S LETTER TO LORD IEYASU FOR ME!
I WILL!
HANBEI, USAGI...
...IT WAS ONLY A SHORT TIME, BUT THANK YOU VERY MUCH FOR THE DELIGHTFUL JOURNEY.
SA...
...SAME HERE...
WHAT...
SWUP
PLEASE TAKE CARE, UNTIL WE MEET AGAIN...

OH.
SNAP
WHA... WHAT...
IT'S A WESTERN WAY OF SAYING GOODBYE.

HUP
SEE YOU!!
WESTERN ...?!
HYAH!
HE REALLY SURPRISED ME THERE...
CLIP CLOP
CLIP CLOP
THAT MAN GOT ON MY NERVES DOWN TO THE VERY LAST MINUTE...
GRR GRR
HANZO...
WHAT IS THIS ABOUT AN ASSASSINATION ATTEMPT ON NOBUNAGA?
PHEW
I MADE IT UP.
YOU MADE IT UP?!
RUSTLE
SORRY!

DON'T TALK ABOUT THAT OUT HERE.
RANMARU WAS TALKING ABOUT AN ATTACK ON IGA!!
BEARDED HANZO...
OH!
HANZOU?!
I DIDN'T HAVE TIME TO EXPLAIN THE SITUATION TO EVERYBODY...
LET'S GO TO LORD IEYASU FIRST...
THIS LETTER FROM LORD NOBUNAGA SAYS THAT THEY'LL BE ATTACKING IGA AT THE BEGINNING OF THE YEAR...
HMM.
TOKUGAWA IEYASU

## UE-RIN'S WAY OF THE MANGA (12)

I had this wily scheme of "It's going to be great if both of my works got accepted for the magazine!" But the words that came out of the editor that I met were...

And so, the editor took the one he liked back with him to Tokyo.
Now that I think about it, he made the right decision. Plus, the other piece that didn't get taken was a good exercise for me, so the work wasn't wasted.

LORD IEYASU...
OFFICIALLY, I'VE FORMED AN ALLIANCE WITH THE ODA FAMILY...
...BUT THE TRUTH IS THAT OKAZAKI IS BASICALLY UNDER LORD NOBUNAGA'S RULE.
GOING AGAINST LORD NOBUNAGA IS EQUIVALENT TO DEATH FOR ME.
THEN WHAT SHOULD WE DO?
I DON'T WANT TO CAUSE YOU ANY DISTRESS.
I'LL DO EVERYTHING I CAN TO HELP YOU.
ONCE I KNOW THE EXACT TIME AND DATE OF THE ATTACK, I'LL CONTACT YOU.

EVEN IF YOU'RE UP AGAINST A LARGE ARMY, YOU MAY BE ABLE TO PLAN TWO OR THREE STEPS AHEAD OF THEM AND FIND A WAY TO EVADE THE ATTACK.
PREPARE YOURSELVES AS BEST YOU CAN.
HANZO...
REALLY, IT'S NOTHING.
LORD IEYASU...
I'M SORRY...
I'M POWER-LESS...
NOT AT ALL.
I'M EXTREMELY GRATEFUL FOR YOUR BENEVOLENCE, LORD IEYASU!!
BY THE WAY...

REALLY...
...HAVE YOU TWO GOTTEN MARRIED?
NO, NOT YET...
HANZO OF IGA...
PLEASE MARRY USAGI AS SOON AS YOU CAN.
I...I INTEND TO DO SO...
DON'T WORRY.
WE'RE GETTING MARRIED AS SOON AS WE RETURN TO IGA!
I'M SO GLAD TO HEAR THAT...
HEE HEE... ♡

LORD IEYASU, THANK YOU FOR EVERY-THING...
USAGI...
IF ANYTHING SHOULD HAPPEN, YOU CAN ALWAYS COME TO MY PLACE.
BUT NOTHING WILL HAPPEN!!
THANK YOU.
MY LORD...
I TRULY APOLOGIZE FOR LEAVING YOU AGAIN.
IT DOESN'T MATTER.
TAKE CARE OF YOURSELF, HANZOU.
I'M SORRY HE'S SUCH A FOOLISH SON...
THANK YOU VERY MUCH FOR YOUR KIND WORDS.

SHE SEEMS SO CARE-FREE...
ISN'T THAT GOOD?
SITUATIONS TEND TO WORK OUT BETTER WHEN YOU HAVE YOUR HEAD UP RATHER THAN DOWN.
...WILL BE WHEN I COME TO TELL YOU THAT WE'VE SAFELY FENDED OFF THE ATTACK.
THE NEXT TIME I'M HERE...
I'M LOOKING FORWARD TO THE GOOD NEWS.
THANK YOU, LORD IEYASU...
TUP

WOOSH
OOOH!
WOOSH
YOU'RE SO FAST!
AT THIS RATE, WE'LL BE BACK IN IGA BY NOON TOMORROW!!
WE'LL BE THERE IN THE MORNING!
ZUFF
MAMEZO...
WOW!!
ONCE WE'RE BACK IN IGA, I NEED YOU TO GO TO HOJIRO TO TELL MASTER TANBA ABOUT THE ATTACK.
OKAY.
AND I'LL GO TELL FUJIBAYASHI.
ZUFF ZUFF

WE MUST DISCUSS DEFENSE MEASURES BETWEEN THE THREE LEADING FAMILIES OF IGA AND COME UP WITH SOMETHING BY THE END OF THE DAY!
IT'S GOING TO BE BUSY...
THE WEDDING...
WHAT'LL HAPPEN TO THE WEDDING?
DON'T WORRY.
HUH?
I PROMISE YOU I'LL FEND OFF THE ATTACK ON IGA NO MATTER WHAT.
BA-BUMP

I BELIEVE YOU, HANZO...
WELL THEN, I'M OFF TO FUJIBAYASHI'S PLACE.
AND I'LL GO FIND MASTER...
YES...
ZUFF
ZUFF
ONCE WE GET BACK, YOU SHOULD GET SOME REST, USAGI.
I BELIEVE YOU.
THERE MUST BE SOMETHING I CAN DO TOO...
!!

MASTER HANZO!!
THE VILLAGE FORTIFICATIONS HAVE CHANGED SO MUCH...!
I'M BACK!

IT'S AS IF A WAR IS GOING TO BREAK OUT ANY MINUTE NOW...
OPEN THE GATE.
MASTER HANZO'S BACK!!

## TAIL OF THE MOON EXTRA: TODAY'S MISSION

"I WANT TO SEE USAGI AND RYO TOGETHER!"

-AOI, KANAGAWA PREFECTURE

SALMON ARE ACTUALLY CONSIDERED TO BE WHITEFISH!
HANZO'S TRIVIA
Tail of the Moon
Chapter 52

WHAT A...
...GRAND-LOOKING STRONGHOLD!!

THE FORTIFICATIONS ARE ALMOST COMPLETE AS YOU ORDERED, MASTER HANZO!
YOU'VE ALL DONE WELL!
WE MUST BUILD THE PERFECT FORTRESS AND KEEP OUR GUARD UP.
WE'RE ALREADY GETTING READY FOR BATTLE?
THAT'S RIGHT.
WE'VE COME BACK TO IGA AT LAST...
WE MUST STOP NOBUNAGA'S ATTACK ON IGA AT ALL COSTS!
...TO TALK TO HANZO ABOUT THE WEDDING...
...BUT THIS IS NO TIME...

WHY DID YOU BRING THE CAT...?
SO THEY'RE GOING TO ATTACK AT THE BEGINNING OF THE YEAR...
PURR
PURR
SOUTH IGA LEADER MOMOCHI TANBA
WE MADE IT THROUGH THE LAST TWO ATTACKS...
...BUT THIS TIME, THEY'RE DEFINITELY GOING TO BRING A HUGE ARMY WITH THEM.
NORTH IGA LEADER NAGATO FUJI-BAYASHI
I FEEL THAT EVERYBODY IN IGA MUST WORK TOGETHER IN ORDER TO FEND OFF THIS ATTACK.

FOR SAMURAI OF THE NORTHERN LANDS, IT MAY BE POSSIBLE...
...BUT DO YOU THINK A SKILLED TACTICIAN LIKE NOBUNAGA WOULD WAGE WAR IN THE WINTER WHEN IT'S SNOWING?
WAIT A MINUTE.
THE LORDS IN THE KINKI REGION WHO ARE UNDER THE CONTROL OF NOBUNAGA WILL LIKELY TAKE PART IN THE ATTACK AS WELL...
YOU'RE RIGHT...
SHOCK
HUH?
...BECAUSE THEIR REAL MOTIVE IS TO ATTACK US BY THE END OF THIS YEAR BEFORE WE'VE HAD A CHANCE TO FULLY PREPARE FOR BATTLE?
WHAT IF THIS RANMARU TOLD YOU THAT THE ATTACK ON IGA WAS GOING TO TAKE PLACE AT THE BEGINNING OF THE YEAR ON PURPOSE...

ARE YOU SAYING THAT RANMARU LIED TO THEM?!
IF HE SAW THROUGH HANZO AND USAGI'S DISGUISES AND FIGURED OUT THEY'RE NINJA, IT'S ENTIRELY POSSIBLE.
EEEP
HE DID NOT SEE THROUGH OUR DISGUISES!
IF HE HAD, WE WOULDN'T HAVE COME BACK ALIVE, RIGHT?
WELL, YOU DO HAVE A POINT THERE, BUT...
IF RANMARU REMEMBERED PASSING BY ME IN KOUGA, THEN HE MAY HAVE KNOWN THAT WE'RE NINJA...
MAYBE I SHOULD TELL THEM ABOUT IT...?

GR...
...GREAT-GRANDPA, I...
OH, I ALMOST FORGOT!
USAGI, SINCE YOU'VE...
...FULFILLED YOUR ASSIGNMENT AT AZUCHI...
...I QUALIFY YOU AS A NINJA!!
REALLY?!

I'M A QUALIFIED NINJA?!
YOU HAVE TO WORK HARD AS A NINJA FROM NOW ON.
I'll do my best!
TH...
WELL DONE, USA...
THANK YOU, GREAT-GRANDPA!!
HMM?
I WANT YOU TO STAY, USAGI.
OKAY!!
I'LL GO AND MAKE A CELEBRATORY FEAST...
WAIT.
HANZO...
CAN WE GET MARRIED RIGHT AWAY?!
Stop it, people are watching...
THE WEDDING WILL OCCUR AFTER ALL OF THIS IS SETTLED.

HANZO...?
SHAAK
YOU GO AND PLAY OUTSIDE, MAMEZO.
MASTER TANBA...
...WHAT IS THAT CAT...
MIIKO IS MY FRIEND.
MEOW!
MAYBE WE'RE GOING TO CONTINUE THAT KISS?!
ALONE IN A ROOM WITH HANZO!!
KEEP YOUR VOICE DOWN.
TROMP TROMP
MMM...
GO AHEAD! ♡
FOLLOW ME.
THERE ARE STAIRS INSIDE THE CLOSET?!
I TOLD YOU TO KEEP YOUR VOICE DOWN!
HUH?
SHUP

OOH...
I NEVER KNEW THERE WAS AN ATTIC...
THIS IS A SECRET ROOM THAT NO ONE KNOWS ABOUT, EVEN THE PEOPLE WHO WORK HERE.
YOU DECIDED TO TELL ME ABOUT SUCH AN IMPORTANT ROOM...
Watch your head.
NO ONE...?
KAMI NO HANZOU KNOWS ABOUT IT...
...BUT THIS ROOM IS ONLY USED BY THE LEADERS OF OUR CLAN.
YOU'RE THE WOMAN WHO IS GOING TO BECOME MY WIFE, USAGI.

ALL THE ANCESTRAL TREASURES AND SECRET SCROLLS ARE KEPT HERE.
THROB
"MY WIFE."
IF ANYTHING SHOULD HAPPEN TO ME, IT WILL BE YOUR JOB TO TAKE CARE OF THEM.
I WON'T DIE AND LEAVE YOU BEHIND.
I'M JUST SAYING "IF"!!
SHUSH!
HANZO, DON'T DIE!!

I WILL SURVIVE THE COMING HARDSHIPS...
...AND MAKE YOU HAPPY, USAGI.
I'M ALREADY HAPPY ENOUGH... ♡
DO NOT TELL ANYONE ABOUT THIS ROOM.
OKAY.
IT'S A SECRET BETWEEN US. ♡

## UE-RIN'S WAY OF THE MANGA 13

During the meeting in Osaka, I got to learn about different tools and techniques from other girls who were there, so it was a really enlightening experience for me.

Since I didn't tell my own friends about drawing manga, meeting people who also drew manga was a great inspiration for me. And so, I continued to draw and send manga and hardly studied for my exams after that. The reason I was still able to attend school without missing classes was because my house was kitty-corner to my school, so I was able to make it in time even if I left my house after the school bell rang.

USAGI...?
I'VE BEEN HIDING THIS FROM YOU ALL THIS TIME, BUT...
ACTUALLY...
...WHEN I WAS KIDNAPPED BY HIKARU...
...I PASSED BY RANMARU IN KOUGA!!
RANMARU DIDN'T SEEM TO REMEMBER ME...
...SO I'VE BEEN PRETENDING NOT TO KNOW ANYTHING ABOUT IT...

BOW
I'M SORRY I DIDN'T TELL YOU UNTIL NOW!!
SCOLD ME, HANZO!!
IT'S ALL MY FAULT...
YOU NEVER CEASE TO SURPRISE ME, USAGI.
...SO SCOLD ME...

IT MUST HAVE BEEN HARD FOR YOU TO TELL ME THAT.
THIS INFORMATION WILL HELP ME COME UP WITH OUR NEXT MOVE.
HUH...
RAISE YOUR HEAD.
ARE...
...AREN'T YOU GOING TO SCOLD ME?
HANZO!!
HANZO...
YOU SURE HAVE SOFTENED UP.

GREAT-GRANDPA?!
IT'S JUST AS I THOUGHT. RANMARU KNEW THAT YOU'RE NINJA!!
IT DOESN'T MEAN THAT HE KNEW ABOUT IT...
IT'S SO OBVIOUS.
IF USAGI REMEMBERED, THEN HE DEFINITELY REMEMBERED AS WELL.
IT ONLY PROVES THAT HE DIDN'T CAPTURE YOU TWO BECAUSE HE WAS GOING TO USE YOU.
YOU MAY BE RIGHT...
HANZO...
THEREFORE, I REVOKE YOUR QUALIFICATION AS A NINJA, USAGI.

YOU TOO, HANZO. YOU SHOULDN'T LOWER YOUR GUARD JUST BECAUSE YOU'VE SMOOCHED USAGI.
SHOCK
HOW DID YOU...
WHAAAAT?!
YOU FAILED YOUR ASSIGNMENT, SO I'M LEFT WITH NO OTHER CHOICE.
I'LL GO TO AZUCHI!
MY WEDDING WITH HANZO JUST KEEPS GETTING TOUGHER AND TOUGHER...
BLUSH
BLUSH
AH!
IT MUST HAVE BEEN MA-MEZO.
Hanzo and Usagi...
SIGH
I GUESS I'LL HAVE TO GO TO AZUCHI MYSELF AND CHECK UP ON RANMARU...

I'LL GO TOO...
NO.
YOU SHOULD STAY HERE AND PRACTICE YOUR NINJUTSU SO THAT YOU CAN RECEIVE YOUR QUALIFICATION.
GOOD!
I'LL GET MY SCOUTS TO WORK WITH YOU.
RECEIVE MY QUALIFICATION...

IF I DON'T GET MY QUALIFICATION, I WON'T BE ABLE TO MARRY HANZO.
YEEEEARGH...
TMP TMP TMP
SCREECH
WHOA, WHOA, WHOA!
THIS TREE SURE DOES GROW FAST...
Even though I broke it, it's already made a comeback.
WELL, YOU HAVE BEEN AWAY FOR A WHILE...
LOOKS LIKE YOU'RE WORKING HARD.
SHA
THAT VOICE...
TUP
!!

HEY.
GOEMON!!
YOU CAN MOVE AROUND ALREADY?!
YAAAY!
YUP!
I TOOK GOOD CARE OF HIM.
OF COURSE.

YURI!!
YOU JUST NEED TO TRY AGAIN, THAT'S ALL.
HOW DID YOU...?
HEARD YOUR QUALIFICATION GOT REVOKED.
OOH...
I'VE BEEN WAITING FOR YOU, GOEMON.
MASTER...
WHAT'S MY NEXT ASSIGNMENT?
ACK!
NINJA WHO LIVE AS NATIVES OF A CERTAIN PLACE IN ORDER TO GATHER INFORMATION.
WHAT'S A "KUSA"?
I WANT YOU TO BECOME A KUSA IN THE CAPITAL...
...AND PREVENT THE ODA ARMY FROM PROCURING WEAPONS.
Duuuh. Idiot.

THE CAPITAL, HUH...
THAT'S GONNA BE TOUGH.
TAKE USAGI WITH YOU ON THIS ASSIGN-MENT.
YOU TWO CAN SNEAK INTO THE CAPITAL POSING AS HUSBAND AND WIFE.
I'M GOING TOO?!
WITH GOEMON THIS TIME...?!
HUSBAND AND WIFE... ♪

YOU'LL BE IN CHARGE OF DELIVERING MESSAGES TO AND FROM THE CAPITAL, MAMEZO.
WITH YOU AGAIN, YUNA?!
I'LL WORK HARD!
YOU'VE GOT AN ASSIGNMENT WITH ME, YURI.
I'LL GO AND POSE AS HIS WIFE...
TUG
HUH?
LET'S GO THEN.
ALREADY ?!
USAGI...
IF YOU FULFILL THIS ASSIGNMENT, I'LL REALLY GIVE YOU YOUR QUALIFICATION.
REALLY?!

I'VE GOT TO DO MY BEST!...
O... OKAY!
LET'S GIVE IT OUR BEST, USAGI. ♪
...SO THAT I CAN MARRY HANZO!!

## TAIL OF THE MOON EXTRA: TODAY'S MISSION

"I WANT TO SEE HANZO AS GUITAR SAMURAI!"

-YOKO HATA, KOUCHI PREFECTURE

BOTH MARGUERITE AND BURDOCK ARE MEMBERS OF THE PLANT FAMILY ASTERACEAE.
HANZO'S TRIVIA
Tail of the Moon
Chapter 53

DEPRESSED
SHFF
SHFF
WE'RE ALMOST THERE.
THIS IS YOUR FIRST TIME TO THE CAPITAL, RIGHT?
TMP
TMP
PULL YOURSELF TOGETHER!!
THE FATE OF IGA DEPENDS ON THIS ASSIGNMENT, YOU KNOW!
SMACK
OW!

...UNDER NORMAL CIRCUMSTANCES, I WOULD HAVE MARRIED HANZO BY NOW...
BUT...
WHAT ARE YOU TALKING ABOUT?!
IF WE CAN'T STOP THE ATTACK ON IGA SOMEHOW, WE'LL ALL BE DEAD BEFORE WE EVEN HAVE THAT WEDDING OF YOURS!!
OH.
THEN PULL YOURSELF TOGETHER!!
I DON'T WANT THAT TO HAPPEN...
I KNOW, BUT...
YOU DON'T HAVE TIME TO BE DEPRESSED!!

I CAN'T BELIEVE I'M POSING AS GOEMON'S WIFE THIS TIME...
GOEMON...
WHAT ARE WE SUPPOSED TO DO AT THE CAPITAL, ANYWAY?

WELL...

LET'S TAKE A REST AT THIS TEAHOUSE FIRST.
SHOCK
A REST ...?!
WELCOME!
WE'LL HAVE TEA AND DUMPLINGS FOR TWO...
...AND...
...A CAT.
CAT ?!

A CAT...
BUT THIS IS A TEA-HOUSE!!
YOU'LL FIND THE CAT ON THE SECOND FLOOR.
Feel free to go up there.
WHAAAAAT?
THEY SELL CATS TOO?!
MEORW
MEORW
HUH?
MIIKO?!
THAT CAT IS MIIKO'S BROTHER, MYAAKO...
...USAGI.
TWITCH
MEORW
MYAAKO, HUH?
...HEY!
HOW COME YOU KNOW MY NAME?!
WE'RE NINJA FROM IGA TOO.

IT'S ALL BEEN SO SUDDEN, SO I HAVEN'T BEEN ABLE TO TELL THE NEIGHBORS.
OOOH...
HAVE YOU BEEN ABLE TO GET EVERYTHING READY?

HUH? WHERE?
LET'S GO, USAGI.
THEN LET'S TAKE CARE OF THAT NOW.

IS THERE ANYTHING YOU NEED?
HEY THERE.
GOOD EVENING.

NINJA ?!
WE'RE KUSA WORKING UNDER MASTER TANBA, AND WE'VE BEEN LIVING IN THE CAPITAL FOR A LONG TIME...
...GATHERING INFORMATION ON THIS PLACE.
"CAT" IS A CODE WE NINJA USE TO IDENTIFY EACH OTHER.

I NEVER KNEW YOU HAD SUCH A HANDSOME SON!
RETIRE?
THIS IS GOEMON AND HIS WIFE USAGI.
I KNOW THIS SEEMS OUT OF THE BLUE...
...BUT WE'RE GOING TO HAND THE SHOP OVER TO OUR SON AND HIS WIFE AND RETIRE.
Wife...
IF YOU EVER NEED A HAND WITH ANYTHING...
...PLEASE FEEL FREE TO ASK ME.
BLUSHooo
I LOOK FORWARD TO SEEING YOU.
ME TOO. ♡
I...I'LL GO AND BUY DUMPLINGS AT YOUR PLACE EVERY DAY. ♡

BY THE WAY, WHEN DID YOU TWO GET MARRIED?
HUH?!
YOU'RE HIS FIANCÉE, AREN'T YOU?
OUR ENGAGEMENT WAS CANCELLED.
USAGI'S NOW THE BRIDE-ELECT OF SEGACHI'S HATTORI HANZO.
BUT WHY?!
YOU TOLD ME IT WAS YOUR DREAM TO MARRY USAGI...
WELL...
...A LOT HAPPENED.
ANYWAY, YOU HAVEN'T FINISHED TEACHING US ALL THE PROCEDURES FOR THIS SHOP YET, SO...
OH, RIGHT.
PEOPLE FROM THE INN LISTED ON THIS ACCOUNT BOOK WILL COME TO BUY DUMPLINGS EVERY MORNING, SO YOU HAVE TO PREPARE THEM BEFORE THE SUN RISES.

DON'T WORRY, USAGI'S REALLY GOOD AT MAKING DUMPLINGS AND TEA.
ALL WE'RE GOING TO DO IS TAKE CARE OF A DUMPLING SHOP?
YOU GET TO HEAR A LOT OF RUMORS AND INFORMATION ABOUT THE CAPITAL FROM THE CUSTOMERS, SO IT'S BEST IF THE SHOP IS THRIVING.
I SEE...
PLEASE KEEP THE SHOP'S REPUTATION UP.
AND TAKE CARE OF MYAAKO FOR US TOO.
WE WILL!

WELL, I'VE GOTTEN A PRETTY GOOD IDEA OF THINGS INSIDE THE HOUSE...
OWW...!
HISSSSS...
SCRATCH
WHAT ARE YOU DOING?
MYAAKO SCRATCHED ME...
JUST LICK IT OR SOMETHING. IT'LL GET BETTER SOON.
OWW!
FWAP
YOU'RE SO MEAN, GOEMON...
LICK
LICK
I'M GOING TO INVESTIGATE THE SITUATION REGARDING NOBUNAGA'S WEAPONS TOMORROW.
NOBUNAGA'S AT AZUCHI, ISN'T HE?
HE OFTEN HOLDS HIS BUSINESS MEETINGS AT HONNOJI, WHICH IS NEAR HERE.
WAIT...DO YOU MEAN NOBUNAGA'S GOING TO BE CLOSE BY?!

IF HE'S PREPARING FOR A LARGE WAR, THEN IT'S A POSSIBILITY.
THEN DOESN'T THAT MEAN RANMARU MAY COME WITH HIM?!
I HAVE TO CHANGE MY HAIRSTYLE!
WHAT'S WITH YOU ALL OF A SUDDEN?
My kimono too...
YOU JUST NEED TO MAKE DUMPLINGS AND SELL THEM.
I WONDER IF I CAN DO IT?
YOU HAVE TO!!
ACK!
NOBUNAGA'S TACTIC IS TOTAL ANNIHILATION...

ANNIHILATION...?
WHEN HE BURNED ENRYAKUJI TO THE GROUND...
...HE MASSACRED EVERYBODY, EVEN THE WOMEN AND CHILDREN.
MASSACRE...
IF YOU DON'T WANT TO DIE, THEN DO YOUR BEST ON THIS ASSIGNMENT!
GLOMP
HEY!
I'M SCARED...

IT HASN'T HAPPENED YET, HAS IT?
I'M SCARED...
I'M GOING TO SLEEP LIKE THIS...!
WHEN ARE YOU GOING TO GET OFF ME?!
I CAN'T WASH MY BACK.
SCRUB SCRUB
TCH.
MNCH MNCH

AAARGH!
GET OFF!!
YOU'RE GOING TO BECOME HANZO'S WIFE, AREN'T YOU?
WHY...?
STOP CLINGING TO ME!!
BUT WE'RE ONLY PRETENDING, AREN'T WE?!
THAT'S TRUE BUT...
...I'M YOUR WIFE AT THE MOMENT, GOEMON...

SNIFF
SNIFF
JUST HURRY UP AND GO TO SLEEP!!
GOEMON HASN'T BEEN HIMSELF TODAY...
I WONDER IF HE'S STRESSED OUT BECAUSE OF THIS ASSIGN-MENT?
NOBUNAGA MAY ACTUALLY BE NEARBY...
I'M SO SCARED...
HANZO...

"HANZO."
"OH..."
"HANZO..."
USAGI.
I'M GOING TO PART WITH YOU.
"PA... PART?!"
YOU HAVE A HUSBAND NAMED GOEMON.
"HUH?!"
"WAIT, HANZO."
GOODBYE, USAGI.
"BUT I'M ONLY PRETENDING TO BE GOEMON'S WIFE..."
Gooood...
...bye...
...bye...
...bye...
WAIT...
WAKE UP, USAGI!!

FLIP
WAKE UP!!
FWUP
NGHH...
FWUP
A DREAM ...?
THANK GOD IT'S ONLY A DREAM...
I'M LEAVING NOW, SO TAKE CARE OF THE SHOP.
THE SHOP!!
DASH
WAARGH
I HAVE TO DO EVERYTHING MYSELF?!
DASH
MAKE THE DUMPLINGS AND THE TEA...
KNEAD KNEAD
OPEN THE SHOP...
GOOD MORNING.

THANK YOU VERY MUCH. ♪
One, two, three...
WHAT...
ARE THOSE DUMPLINGS ?!
I'D LIKE TO HAVE THIRTY OF THE USUAL DUMPLINGS.
ANYWAY...
THIRTY?!
GOO... GOOD MORNING!
ARE YOU THE NEW SHOPKEEPER?
YOU LOOK REALLY YOUNG. CAN YOU HANDLE THIS PLACE?
TH...THIS IS THE ONLY TYPE OF DUMPLING I MAKE...
I DIDN'T ASK FOR THOSE SIMPLE COUNTRY-STYLE DUMPLINGS! WHERE ARE THE USUAL ONES?!
UM...
HAVE YOU GOTTEN USED TO YOUR SURROUNDINGS YET?
GOOD MORNING.
WAIT...!
FORGET IT! I'LL BUY THEM AT ANOTHER SHOP!!
H... HEY...
SHUP

It was a waste of time to dress up...
WHAT? WE CAME ALL THE WAY HERE TO SEE HIS GORGEOUS FACE FOR NOTHING?
WE DON'T WANT ANY!!
UM... HOW ABOUT SOME DUMPLINGS?
BEAM
BEAM
OH...
IT'S YOU TWO...
SO WHERE'S YOUR FINE HUSBAND?
GOEMON'S GONE OUT FOR THE MOMENT...
CAN'T YOU BUY...
...AT LEAST ONE DUMPLING?
It wouldn't hurt...
...to buy just one...
WHAT SHOULD I DO?
I HAVEN'T BEEN ABLE TO SELL EVEN ONE DUMPLING SINCE THIS MORNING...
DUMPLINGS
Ira Shop
"PLEASE KEEP THE SHOP'S REPUTATION UP."
"PAY ATTENTION TO WHAT THE CUSTOMERS SAY."
MY ASSIGNMENT...
ARE YOU OPEN?

WELCOME!!
TEA FOR TWO.
SURE THING!
COMING RIGHT UP!!
I HAVE TO WORK HARD SO THAT THEY'LL LIKE THIS SHOP. ♪
OOPS.
CRASH
LOOK AT THIS WONDERFUL TEA BOWL.
THIS SHOP IS RATHER NOISY...
OOH...
IT SHOULD BE YOUR FAMILY TREASURE FROM NOW ON.
I KNOW. ♪
HUFF HUFF
SORRY TO HAVE KEPT YOU WAITING.

TEE HEE ♡
IT'S ON THE HOUSE. ♡
HERE YOU ARE. ♡
PLOP
I DIDN'T ORDER ANY DUMPLINGS.
SPLASH SPLASH
LET ME...
...POUR THE TEA FOR YOU.
HEY, THIS IS...
IT'S HOT!
WHOA.

OW
OW
I'M SO SORRY...
HOW...
!!
SHATTER
HOW DARE YOU...
...SMASH THE PRECIOUS TEA BOWL THAT I RECEIVED FROM LORD NOBUNAGA...?
UH...

NOBU...?
SHIN AN
IT'S UN-FORGIVABLE !!
AAAAARGH

YOU...
YOU'RE GOING TO BE THE ONE IN A FIX IF YOU CAUSE TROUBLE IN THE CAPITAL, SADANARI.
TREMBLE
TREMBLE
PLEASE STOP THAT.
GRAB
BUT...
...THIS GIRL BROKE THE TEA BOWL I RECEIVED FROM LORD NOBUNAGA...
ANYTHING THAT HAS A SHAPE WILL PERISH SOMEDAY.
AND I'M SURE THIS GIRL DIDN'T BREAK THE BOWL ON PURPOSE, RIGHT?
THAT VOICE...

IF YOU SAY SO, RANMARU...
MISS...
ARE YOU OKAY?
RANMARU?!

## TAIL OF THE MOON EXTRA: TODAY'S MISSION

"I WANT TO SEE USAGI AS A MAID!"

-AKIHABARA, YAMANASHI PREFECTURE

Tail of the Moon
Chapter 54
THE KING CRAB IS A TYPE OF HERMIT CRAB.
HANZO'S TRIVIA

MISS...
WHY IS RANMARU HERE?!
...HAVE WE MET SOMEWHERE BEFORE?

STOP TALKING LIKE THAT.
SCREECH
SCREECH
I...
I'VE NEVER MET YOU BEFORE!!
!!
LET ME SEE YOUR FACE.
AAAGH... I'VE GOT NO OTHER CHOICE NOW...
WHY ARE YOU HIDING YOUR FACE?
I'M... TOO... SHY...
...YOU... YOU'RE SO BEAUTIFUL...
BECAUSE...
SCREECH
SCREECH
IS THAT SO?
YOU WERE TALKING TO US WITH YOUR MOUTH WIDE OPEN A MINUTE AGO...
WHY YOU...
PAY FOR IT?!
YOU'RE GOING TO PAY FOR THE TEA BOWL!!

WHAAAAT?!
...IT WON'T BE ENOUGH EVEN IF YOU SELL THIS DIRTY SHOP OF YOURS!!
WHAT'S WITH ALL THIS NOISE?
HOW... HOW MUCH IS IT?
I CAN'T PUT A PRICE ON A TEA BOWL GIVEN TO ME BY LORD NOBUNAGA, BUT...
ODA CLAN RETAINER MITSUHIDE AKECHI
MITSUHIDE!!
I CAN HEAR YOUR VOICE FROM OUTSIDE, SADANARI.
OHH...
THIS GIRL BROKE THE TEA BOWL THAT I RECEIVED FROM LORD NOBUNAGA!

## UE-RIN'S WAY OF THE MANGA (14)

Back then, I had extracurricular activities, so I would swim three kilometers after school every day. I also attended cram school twice a week and was even learning calligraphy and piano during the weekends. I had to cut my sleeping time in order to draw my manga. Basically, the time I had to draw manga was very precious to me.

I hadn't made my debut yet, but I had an editor who would take a look at my manga and fix certain areas before it was submitted to a magazine. This happened to be a very stressful thing for me.

And the reason for that was...

YOU JUST NEED TO BE MORE CAREFUL NEXT TIME.
THANK YOU VERY MUCH FOR HELPING ME!!
BOW
OW.
BANG
I...I'M ALIVE...
HAHAHA, IT'S NOTHING.
ARE YOU OKAY, MITSUHIDE?
WHAT HAPPENED HERE?!
IF RANMARU'S HERE AT THE CAPITAL, THEN...!!
I CAN'T REST EASY YET!!
I GUESS THERE ARE SOME NICE PEOPLE AMONG NOBUNAGA'S VASSALS...
OH!

WHAT HAPPENED?!
I WAS SO SCARED...
GOEMON...
SO...
THIS RANMARU GUY DIDN'T NOTICE IT WAS YOU, DID HE?
AND WHEN ARE YOU GOING TO GET OFF ME?!
I'M STILL SCARED...
DON'T BE SUCH A BABY.
OWW!
YOU SHOULD STAY INSIDE STARTING TO-MORROW, USAGI.
I WILL.
RANMARU THINKS I'M HANBEI'S WIFE FROM OKAZAKI!!

WHY ARE YOU SO COLD TO ME?!
IT'S NOT LIKE YOU, GOEMON.
HAVE I DONE SOMETHING WRONG?!
NO YOU HAVEN'T, USAGI...
WAAAAH...
THEN WHY...
WE DON'T HAVE TIME TO TALK ABOUT THAT RIGHT NOW.
NOBUNAGA IS AT HONNOJI AS WE SPEAK!

I TOOK A LOOK AT HONNOJI...
...BUT IT'S HEAVILY GUARDED WITH NOBUNAGA THERE, SO I'M NOT GOING TO BE ABLE TO SNEAK IN THAT EASILY.
WE'RE GOING TO HAVE TO USE THE DUMPLING SHOP.
WE'RE GOING TO GO IN THERE...?
THAT'S OUR JOB, ISN'T IT?
HEY, SO HOW MANY DUMPLINGS DID YOU SELL TODAY?
NOT EVEN ONE... YET...
YOU COULDN'T SELL ANY?!
YOU'RE KIDDING ME, RIGHT?

STEP RIGHT UP, STEP RIGHT UP!
HEY, PRETTY GIRL, WHY DON'T YOU DROP BY AND HAVE ONE?
THE DUMPLING SHOP "USAGI" JUST OPENED, SO WE'RE HAVING A SALE TODAY.
TMP TMP TMP
I'LL BUY ONE...
ME TOO... ♡
THIS DUMPLING DOESN'T LOOK VERY GOOD, BUT IT TASTES GREAT.
YES, OF COURSE!
COULD YOU HAVE TEN OF THEM WRAPPED UP FOR ME TO TAKE HOME?
The tea's delicious too...
USAGI, ARE THE DUMPLINGS READY YET?
I'M GLAD YOU'RE SELLING SO MANY, BUT I'M THE ONLY ONE WHO'S MAKING THEM, Y'KNOW!
ROLL ROLL
SLURP

THIS DUMPLING SHOP SEEMS REALLY POPULAR.
LET'S GIVE IT A TRY.
WAITER, COULD YOU REFILL MY TEA?
COMING!
WHERE ARE OUR DUMPLINGS ?
THEY'LL BE HERE IN A MINUTE...
HEY!
STOP CUTTING IN LINE.
OH, NO.
AREN'T YOU THE ONE WHO'S CUTTING?!
MA'AM...
WE'RE CURRENTLY HANDING OUT NUMBERED TICKETS, SO PLEASE WAIT UNTIL YOUR NUMBER IS CALLED!

YURI?!
I THOUGHT YOU COULD USE SOME HELP. ♡
PLEASE LINE UP WITHOUT BLOCKING THE WAY OF THE OTHER CUSTOMERS.
HERE YOU ARE.
LET ME REFILL YOUR TEA.
THANKS, YURI.
OOH ♡
ANYTHING FOR YOU, GOEMON.
SHE'S EFFICIENT AND PRETTY. YOU SHOULD HAVE MARRIED A GIRL LIKE HER, GOEMON...
WELL, IT'S NOT THAT EASY...
HA HA HA
THAT'S WHY I'M HERE!
HAHAHAHA
THEY SEEM TO BE HAVING A LOT OF FUN OUT THERE...
HUFF
HUFF

DID I DO A GOOD JOB?
YOU DID, YOU DID!
I'M EXHAUSTED...
AT THIS RATE, WE MIGHT EVEN START GETTING CUSTOMERS FROM HONNOJI.

NICE WORK, BOTH OF YOU!!

WITH YURI AROUND, I FEEL A LOT MORE COMFORTABLE BEING AWAY FROM THE SHOP.
WHAT...

I'M GOING TO BE LEAVING FOR SAKAI RIGHT AWAY, SO I NEED YOU TWO TO TAKE CARE OF THE SHOP FOR A WHILE.
WHAAAT?

BUT...
YURI...
I'M COUNTING ON YOU.
YES, SIR! ♡
GOEMON...
I'LL BE BACK.
DON'T WORRY.
SHHHK
OKAY...

WHY ARE YOU ALWAYS THE ONE WHO GETS GOEMON'S ATTENTION?!
BOOF
AAAH
THIS IS SO FRUSTRATING!
YURI, I'M LOOKING FORWARD TO WORKING WITH YOU TOMORROW...
DON'T YOU UNDERSTAND THE REASON FOR HIM SMILING AT YOU JUST NOW?!
HE'S BEEN REALLY MEAN TO ME LATELY...
GOEMON WASN'T GIVING ME ATTENTION...
I DON'T WANT TO TALK TO A STUPID PERSON LIKE YOU ANYMORE!!
HUH... WAS HE SMILING?
...
ZZZ...

SHHK
HANZO...
I WONDER WHAT YOU'RE DOING RIGHT NOW?
"...AND MAKE YOU HAPPY, USAGI."
"I WILL SURVIVE THE COMING HARD-SHIPS..."

I WANT TO MAKE HANZO HAPPY TOO...
...WITH ALL MY MIGHT...
THREE DAYS LATER
USAGI...
I'VE GOT BIG NEWS.
WHAT'S GOING ON?
A...A MESSENGER FROM HONNOJI JUST CAME AND ASKED US TO DELIVER THEM SOME DUMPLINGS!!
HONNOJI...
YOU SHOULD GO TO HONNOJI AND INVESTIGATE THAT PLACE.
WHAT?

NO WAY!
YOU GO, YURI.
I HAVE TO SERVE THE CUSTOMERS AT THIS SHOP.
BUT...
...RANMARU MIGHT BE AT HONNOJI...
JUST DISGUISE YOURSELF SO THAT HE WON'T RECOGNIZE YOU. ♪
PAT
DISGUISE?!

DON'T YOU WANT TO GET THIS ASSIGNMENT OVER WITH QUICKLY SO THAT YOU CAN RETURN TO IGA?
YES, BUT...
IF HANZO HEARS ABOUT THIS, I BET HE'LL PRAISE YOU FOR IT.
HANZO WILL?!

I CAN'T BELIEVE USAGI DID A RECONNAISSANCE OF HONNOJI!!
WHAT AN AMAZING ACCOMPLISHMENT...
...THAT MY LOVELY BRIDE-ELECT FULFILLED!!

NOW YOU CAN BE QUALIFIED AS A NINJA. ALL WE'VE GOT LEFT IS THE WEDDING.
OH, HANZO. ♡

NOW DON'T FORGET TO STAY AT HONNOJI AS LONG AS YOU CAN AND MEMORIZE THE ROOM LOCATIONS AND THE NUMBER OF PEOPLE WHO ARE THERE, OKAY?
SMOOOOCH
OOH, JUST IMAGINE THAT... ♡
I'LL DO IT!!
HEY...
DON'T MOVE!!
You've made me mess up the rouge on your lips...

WELL, YOU HARDLY HAVE ANY CHARM SO I HAD TO MAXIMIZE WHAT FEW ASSETS YOU HAVE.
ISN'T THIS A LITTLE TOO SHOWY?
OW!
SLAP
JUST MAKE SURE YOU FULFILL YOUR ASSIGN-MENT.
MAYBE I LOOK STRANGE TO THEM.
EVERYBODY'S LOOKING AT ME...

EXCUSE ME...
CAN YOU TELL ME WHERE HONNOJI IS?
TH-THUMP
TH-THUMP
HUH?
COME TO THINK OF IT...
...WHERE EXACTLY IS HONNOJI, ANYWAY?!
TH-THUMP
TH-THUMP
AAAGH, I'M SO NERVOUS...
TH-THUMP
TH-THUMP
COME ON, I CAN DO THIS...
YOU'RE STANDING RIGHT IN FRONT OF IT.
OH!
WHAT DO YOU WANT?
UM...
I...I CAME TO DELIVER DUMPLINGS...
TH-THUMP
TH-THUMP
WHO ORDERED THEM?
HUH?

RAN...
OH, RANMARU.
COME ON, SPIT IT OUT.
I DON'T KNOW WHO...!!
THINK! THINK!
AND THEN THERE'S...
I can't say that Sada-whatever guy...
What was that nice person called?!
WHO'S HERE AGAIN?
I'LL GO GET HIM THEN.
NOT RANMARU...
OH!
HEY, RANMARU!
VIP
I'LL TELL HIM TO COME OVER, SO JUST WAIT HERE.
GASP
GASP
YOU'RE TURNING RED.
TH... THAT'S OKAY...
AH-HA! YOU MUST HAVE A CRUSH ON RANMARU, RIGHT?
TUG
EEEK

...BUT HOW AM I SUPPOSED TO INVESTIGATE WITH ALL THESE PEOPLE...?
I'VE GOTTEN INSIDE HONNOJI...
TH-THUMP
TH-THUMP
IF RANMARU SEES ME, IT'S GOING TO RUIN EVERYTHING...
!!
YOU THERE.
WHAT ARE YOU DOING?
HEY, WAIT!!
TMP
DASH...
EEEEEEEK
AAARGH! IT'S THAT TEA BOWL GUY!!
WHERE HAVE I SEEN YOU BEFORE...?
HUH?

YEAH, RIGHT!!
COME BACK HERE!!
OH, SHOOT!
!!
THUNK
WATCH OUT!
AAH!!
GRAB

FLUMP
YOU'RE...!!

TAIL OF THE MOON EXTRA: TODAY'S MISSION

"I WANT TO SEE HANZO AS A TEACHER IN SCHOOL!"

-TOMOPYON, HOKKAIDO

KETCHUP ORIGINATED IN CHINA.
HANZO'S TRIVIA
Tail of the Moon
Chapter 55

TMP
RANMARU...
TMP
YOU'RE...!!
STOP THAT SUSPICIOUS WOMAN!!
OH, NO.
TUG

WHAT DO YOU MEAN, SUSPICIOUS?
SHE'S MY GIRLFRIEND.
GIRL-FRIEND?!
YOUR GIRL-FRIEND, RAN-MARU?!
YES.
PLEASE DON'T TELL LORD NOBUNAGA ABOUT IT.
SHUP
!
JINGLE
VERY WELL...
I didn't see any-thing.
RA... RANMARU ?!
LET'S GO TO MY ROOM FIRST.

KEE!
KEE...
MOSUKE?!
JOLT
SO IT IS YOU, USAGI. JUST AS I SUSPECTED.
OH NO OH NO OH NO!
I THOUGHT YOU WENT BACK TO OKAZAKI. WHY ARE YOU AT THE CAPITAL?
OH NO OH NO OH NO OH NO OH NO OH NO!
WHAT'S WRONG?
KEE?
OHHH...
OH...

I'M SORRY, HANZO...
JEEZ, IT SOUNDS LIKE A LIE, EVEN TO ME!
...I'VE DIVORCED HANBEI...AND I'M CURRENTLY RUNNING A DUMPLING SHOP HERE IN THE CAPITAL...
TO TELL YOU THE TRUTH...

I KNEW IT! IT'S TOO OBVIOUS...
AAAGH...
DIVORCE?!

THEN DID YOU MAKE THESE DUMPLINGS?
OH, THANK GOD!
TH... THAT'S RIGHT!!

RANMARU...
I NEED TO TALK TO YOU ABOUT THE TEA CEREMONY TOMORROW...
WE'LL HAVE THESE LATER THEN.
UH... UH-HUH!

SO THAT'S WHY YOU WERE HIDING YOUR FACE AT THE DUMPLING SHOP!!
WHA—?

IT'S THAT BITTER OLD MAN WHO LIKES TEA!!
OH?
OH! IS SHE GOING TO BE ATTENDING LORD NOBUNAGA'S TEA CEREMONY TOMORROW?
MASTER RIKYU...
REMEMBER USAGI? YOU MET HER BACK IN AZUCHI.
OH, USAGI...
WHAT?!
WOULD YOU MIND TEACHING ME HOW TO MAKE THAT DELICIOUS TEA OF YOURS?
I've brought tea leaves and tools along with me.
TEA CEREMONY ?!
WE FINALLY GET TO HAVE HER MEET LORD NOBUNAGA.
YES.

OH... OKAY...
SKRTCH
SKRTCH
THEN PLEASE WRITE THE INGREDIENTS DOWN.
I'LL HAVE THEM FETCHED.
I...I DON'T USE REGULAR TEA LEAVES FOR THAT TEA...
BUT...
PLEASE WAIT HERE FOR A WHILE.
I'LL GO AND HAVE THESE PREPARED RIGHT AWAY!
OH
ZWAK
WSP
WSP
THIS ATTACK ON IGA...
WHAT?
WHAT SHOULD I DO?

PRESS
ATTACK ON IGA?!
KEE?
I'VE HEARD THAT IT'S GOING TO BE LED BY LORD NOBUKATSU.
WE DIDN'T SUCCEED LAST TIME, SO HE'S GOING TO TRY AND WIN THIS BATTLE AT ALL COSTS.
I HEARD THAT WE'RE GOING TO ATTACK FROM ALL FOUR DIRECTIONS.
THAT'S RIGHT...
FROM AOYAMA TOUGE, TAMATAKIGUCHI, KASAMAGUCHI AND...
...LET'S SEE...
I'VE GOT TO WRITE THESE NAMES DOWN!
...OTOGI TOUGE.
I CAN'T WRITE PROPERLY WITH MY HANDS SHAKING!!
TREMBLE
TREMBLE
TREMBLE
TREMBLE
AOYAMA
TO

JUST WHEN...
WE'LL ALL BE KILLED!!
...I FINALLY CONNECTED WITH HANZO...
IF THEY ATTACK US FROM ALL FOUR DIRECTIONS, WE'LL NEVER WIN.
GRAB

I'M GOING TO PROTECT HANZO!!
GREAT-GRANDPA, GRANDPA...
...AND EVERYBODY ELSE AT IGA... I CAME ALL THE WAY HERE TO PROTECT THEIR HAPPINESS.
...MAMEZO...
...SO WHY DON'T YOU STAY HERE AND HAVE DINNER WITH US?
YE... YES?
IT'S GOING TO TAKE SOME TIME FOR ALL THE TEA INGREDIENTS TO BE READY...
ZWAK
NOW'S THE TIME TO DO MY BEST...
USAGI.

YES, SIR.
WE HAVE A GUEST FOR DINNER, SO PLEASE PREPARE ONE MORE MEAL.
TMP
TMP
DUMP
DUMP

HUH?
MASTER RIKYU...
IT'S RUDE TO BUTT IN ON OTHER PEOPLE'S RELATIONSHIPS...
BY THE WAY, USAGI...
...WHEN DID YOU AND RANMARU BECOME LOVERS?
PEOPLE'S MINDS CAN CHANGE VERY EASILY.
BUT ONLY A WHILE AGO, USAGI WAS...
USAGI, DON'T YOU LIKE THE FOOD?
THIS CRISPY THING'S REALLY DELICIOUS!!
NO, I DO.
CRNCH
CRNCH
IT'S A WESTERN DISH CALLED TEMPURA.
SADANARI MURAI. MITSUHIDE AKECHI.
I'VE LEARNED THEIR NAMES AT LAST.
NOW THAT I'M IN THIS SITUATION, I'M GOING TO DO AS MUCH INVESTIGATING AS POSSIBLE !!
IT'S PROBABLY SOMETHING A DEVOTED HUSBAND LIKE MITSUHIDE WILL NEVER BE ABLE TO UNDERSTAND.
YOU'RE RIGHT. I DON'T UNDER-STAND.

MITSU-HIDE...
YOU'RE NOT FEELING WELL?
I'M GOING TO GO TO BED.
YEAH...
I'm not too fond of fried food...
COULD YOU EAT MINE TOO THEN?
HE MUST STILL BE SHAKEN FROM BEING CRITICIZED BY LORD NOBUNAGA YESTERDAY.
NOW THAT YOU MENTION IT...
...IS IT TRUE THAT THE SCAR ON HIS FOREHEAD IS FROM BEING ATTACKED BY LORD NOBUNAGA?
THAT'S RIGHT.
LORD NOBUNAGA WAS ENRAGED WHEN MITSUHIDE DIDN'T PICK UP THE GRAIN OF RICE LORD NOBUNAGA HAD DROPPED ON THE FLOOR...
JUST FOR THAT?!

LORD NOBUNAGA'S LIKE A GOD NOW.
SADANARI...
DON'T FORGET THAT WE HAVE A GUEST!
WELL, WHATEVER THE REASON, IT'S BECAUSE HE'S BEEN MESSING UP A LOT LATELY, ISN'T IT?
WHAT ARE YOU TALKING ABOUT? MITSUHIDE IS A FINE MILITARY COMMANDER.
I KNOW THAT A LOT OF PEOPLE ARE JEALOUS OF HIM FOR BEING PROMOTED SO QUICKLY.
I AM NOT JEALOUS OF HIM!!
FOR SIMPLY NOT PICKING UP A GRAIN OF RICE, NOBUNAGA DID SUCH A CRUEL THING...
USAGI...
I'D LIKE YOU TO STAY HERE FOR THE NIGHT.

## UE-RIN'S WAY OF THE MANGA 15

Back then, household fax machines, convenience stores, and door-to-door delivery service weren't that common. That's why I would photocopy my storyboard at the local stationery store for 30 yen per page, send it by express mail, and wait for a reply to come. Unfortunately, the reply from the editor always took a long time. I kept worrying, thinking things like, "Maybe it didn't reach them because of some accident..." Even though I wanted to call to see if my storyboard got there okay, I was kind of scared and embarrassed...

(It was expensive!)

I never did call them in the end.

The long waiting time felt like such a waste of time to me...

THAT IDIOT.
WHY HASN'T SHE COME BACK YET?!
OOH
WAIT 'TIL I GET MY HANDS ON HER!
SHOCK
I...I'M GOING TO BE SLEEPING NEXT TO YOU, RANMARU?
KEE.
THIS IS MOSUKE'S FUTON, SO WE'LL USE THAT FUTON TOGETHER...
BUT I CAN'T DO THAT...
YUP

WE'RE LOVERS.
WHY NOT?
YOU'RE EVEN CUTER WHEN YOU BLUSH. ♡
TUG
BUT WE'RE FAKE LOVERS, RIGHT?!
JUST KIDDING. ♪
GUH...?!
HE REALLY SCARED ME THERE...
GASP GASP
DON'T FORGET TO BLOW OUT THE LIGHT BEFORE YOU GO TO SLEEP.
I'LL SLEEP WITH MOSUKE.
KEE.

MY STOMACH HURTS TOO...
THAT TEMPURA WAS REALLY GOOD, BUT I ATE TOO MUCH OF IT...
I NEED TO TAKE SOME MEDICINE...
RUSTLE
HOW CAN I POSSIBLY SLEEP IN A SITUATION LIKE THIS?!
I'M TOO NERVOUS TO FALL ASLEEP.
OH.
WHAT'S THE MATTER?
WHY ARE YOU UP SO LATE?
A LIGHT...
MAYBE THIS IS THE KITCHEN?

I'M SORRY I ASKED YOU TO EAT MY PORTION AS WELL.
TEMPURA IS A DELICACY, BUT IT IS RATHER HEAVY FOR THE STOMACH...
TP
WELL...MY STOMACH HURTS, SO I WAS GOING TO TAKE SOME MEDICINE...
IT MUST BE THE TEMPURA.
HERE, I'LL POUR YOU SOME WATER.

HEY...
IS SOMETHING WRONG WITH YOUR EYES?
MITSUHIDE...
YOU'RE SPILLING IT...
AAH!
SPLASH

SORRY...
I'VE BEEN TRYING NOT TO LET ANYONE FIND OUT ABOUT MY EYES...
AH!
I'M SORRY...
SHIVER
SHIVER
DON'T TELL ANYONE ABOUT THIS!!
TREMBLE
I MADE IT.
WHERE IS IT FROM?
IT RELIEVES FATIGUE, BUT IT ALSO HELPS REFRESH THE EYES...
WHY DON'T YOU TRY THIS MEDICINE?
I WAS AN HERBALIST FOR LORD IEYASU FOR A SHORT TIME...
YOU DID?

THANK YOU.
THEN I CAN TAKE IT WITHOUT ANY WORRIES.
AN HERBALIST FOR LORD IEYASU?!
UH... UH-HUH...
MAYBE I SHOULDN'T HAVE SAID THAT...?!
GOOD NIGHT...
PHEW
I'M GLAD HE'S HAPPY.
...
BUT WE'RE NOT REALLY LOVERS...
BUT...
YOU SHOULD RETURN TO YOUR ROOM QUICKLY TOO.
RANMARU WILL BE WORRIED ABOUT YOU.
I CAN TAKE YOU TO YOUR ROOM IF YOU WANT.
MITSUHIDE'S EYES SEEM TO BE PRETTY BAD.
THERE'S NO NEED.

WE'RE HAVING A TEA CEREMONY WITH NOBUNAGA TOMORROW TOO...
HUH?
BUT AM I EVEN GOING TO BE ABLE TO RETURN TO IGA?!
ONCE I GO BACK TO IGA, I'LL TRY AND MAKE SOME MEDICINE THAT WILL CURE EYE PROBLEMS...
WHERE DID RANMARU GO...?
HUG
EEEEK!

I WAS WORRIED SINCE YOU WEREN'T AROUND WHEN I WOKE UP.
STOP JOKING AROUND!!
IS IT THAT much FUN TO TEASE ME?
...
?!
RANMARU ?!
IT'S NOT FUN AT ALL.

THE NOTE I WROTE ABOUT THE ATTACK ON IGA!!
DANGLE
KASA OTOGI TOU
IF SOMEBODY ELSE HAD FOUND THIS...
I FOUND THIS ON THE FLOOR.
...YOU WOULD HAVE BEEN...
...DEAD BY NOW...
CRUMPLE

...MISS KUNOICHI FROM IGA.

## TAIL OF THE MOON EXTRA: TODAY'S MISSION

"I WANT TO SEE HANZO IN SCHOOLWEAR!"

-KIMIKA, HOKKAIDO

"PLUS ALPHA" IS JAPANESE ENGLISH, SO IT DOESN'T MAKE SENSE IN ANY ENGLISH-SPEAKING COUNTRY.
HANZO'S TRIVIA
Tail of the Moon
Chapter 56

THE KOUGA NINJA ARE TAKING PART IN THE ATTACK AS WELL...?
THEY'RE NOT GOING TO BE PARTICI-PATING IN THE BATTLE ITSELF...
...BUT THEY HAVE ACCEPTED THE ROLE OF LEADING THE ARMY DOWN TO IGA.
THEY WERE SCARED THAT THEY'D MEET THE SAME FATE AS IGA IF THEY DIDN'T COOPERATE...

ZWAK
USAGI IS AT THE CAPITAL?!
!!
DIDN'T YOU GET ANYTHING FROM USAGI? SHE'S AT THE CAPITAL, AFTER ALL.
SUZUNE...
HOW LARGE WILL THE ARMY BE, AND WHEN WILL THEY ATTACK?
I DON'T KNOW YET...
DIDN'T YOU KNOW, HANZO?
THIS IS THE FIRST TIME I'VE HEARD ABOUT IT!
YOU AMATEUR...
SHE'S WORKING AS A KUSA, POSING AS GOEMON'S WIFE AT A TEAHOUSE NEAR HONNOJI.
I CAN'T BELIEVE YOU DON'T KEEP TRACK OF YOUR BRIDE-ELECT'S MOVEMENTS...

...
HANZO?
HMMMMPH
ZZZ
DON'T RAISE YOUR VOICE.
YOU'RE GOING TO WAKE MOSUKE UP.
NOD
NOD
IF YOU PROMISE ME THAT YOU WON'T YELL, I'LL TAKE MY HAND AWAY.

GASP
I'VE NEVER MET A NINJA AS CARELESS AS YOU.
THIS IS SUCH OBVIOUS PROOF...
RIP
RIP
BUT YOU'VE BEEN CARELESS FROM THE FIRST TIME WE MET, BACK AT AZUCHI...
YOU NOTICED BACK THEN?!
YES.
IF HE KNEW I WAS A NINJA FROM IGA ALL THIS TIME, WHY DIDN'T HE KILL ME...?
NEVERTHELESS, YOU'RE STILL GOING TO MAKE TEA FOR LORD NOBUNAGA TOMORROW.
EH?

PLEASE REFRAIN FROM MAKING ANY STUPID MOVES.
BOOSH
AAAH
DON'T FORGET...
...YOUR LIFE IS IN MY HANDS.
VUP
WELL THEN, GOOD NIGHT.

WHAT DOES THIS MEAN?!
"DON'T FORGET YOUR LIFE IS IN MY HANDS."
IS HE GOING TO KILL ME IF I TRY TO RUN?!
BUT I HAVE TO TAKE THAT INFORMATION ABOUT THE ATTACK BACK TO IGA.
WHAT SHOULD I DO, HANZO?!

I'VE PREPARED THE THINGS YOU NEED FOR YOUR TEA!!
USAGI...
...THANK YOU...
TH...
THERE ISN'T ANYTHING STRANGE MIXED WITH THESE HERBS, IS THERE?
MASTER RIKYU...
USAGI, YOUR EYES ARE RED. DIDN'T YOU GET ANY SLEEP?
Y... YEAH.
A LITTLE...

HOW RUDE OF YOU!
ALL OF THESE PLANTS ARE HARMLESS.
ISN'T THAT RIGHT, USAGI?!
RI... RIGHT.
OH!
THIS HERB!!
IS...IS THERE SOMETHING BAD...?
NOT AT ALL.
I'LL BE ABLE TO MAKE THE USUAL TEA WITH THESE.
I'M GOING DOWN TO GET LORD NOBUNAGA, SO PLEASE TAKE CARE OF EVERYTHING ELSE.

SHHHK
I MIGHT BE ABLE TO GET OUT OF THIS SITUATION...
...AND RETURN TO HANZO'S SIDE!!
THIS IS REALLY ENCOURAG-ING...
THAT'S THE SPIRIT, USAGI!!

NO!
LET ME GET A TASTE OF IT...
SLAP
IT'S BEGINNING TO SMELL GREAT.
OOH...
AAH...
I CAN'T LET THEM FIND OUT!!
Y...YOU'RE GOING TO INTERFERE WITH THE FLAVOR OF THE TEA, SO DON'T TOUCH IT!
OUCH...
PLEASE DO...
OH...
OF COURSE...
THEN I'M GOING TO HAVE TO VISIT YOUR SHOP "USAGI" EVERY DAY.
CAN IT BE...
...THAT YOUR TEA TASTES DIFFERENT EACH TIME?!

YURI'S ALL ALONE AT THE SHOP!
IF RANMARU KNOWS THAT I'M A NINJA, THEN HE KNOWS ABOUT THE SHOP TOO!!
CLOSED TEMPORARY Usagi
OH, THEY'RE CLOSED TODAY...
WHAT A PITY.

SHUNK
UM...
AREN'T WE GOING TO START THE TEA CEREMONY?

WE HAVE SOME NOBLES ATTENDING THIS EVENT, SO WE REALLY CAN'T POSTPONE IT EITHER...
OH...
WE CAN'T START UNTIL LORD NOBUNAGA ARRIVES.
WHY ARE YOU IN A RUSH TO START?
THEN LET'S GET IT OVER WITH...
BECAUSE IT'S BETTER WITHOUT NOBUNAGA OR RANMARU AROUND!!
UM...
I... UH...
TMP
TMP
LORD NOBUNAGA WILL NOT BE ATTENDING THE TEA CEREMONY TODAY.
I'M VERY SORRY.
WHAT?!

WE CAN'T DO IT WITHOUT THE HOST, CAN WE...
LET'S DO IT.
HE SAID HE WON'T ATTEND BECAUSE "THE WIND IS BLOWING FROM THE SOUTHEAST THIS MORNING."
WHAT'S THAT SUPPOSED TO MEAN?!
THEN WHAT ABOUT THE CEREMONY?
I'VE ALREADY MADE THE TEA FOR THIS OCCASION...
...AND THERE ARE A LOT OF GUESTS WAITING...
WOOOOO
ICHIJO NO KIMI...
HMM...
DON'T YOU THINK IT'S RATHER RUDE OF THE HOST TO BE ABSENT WHEN HE ASKED US TO ATTEND A TEA CEREMONY OUTSIDE ON A COLD DAY LIKE THIS?

YOU'VE BEEN UNUSUALLY SILENT TODAY, ICHIJO NO KIMI.
COUGH
HRMM...
I'M SORRY TO HAVE KEPT YOU WAITING.
HERE YOU ARE. DRINK IT WHILE IT'S STILL HOT.
WHAT IS THIS?
AREN'T YOU GOING TO BREW THE TEA LIKE YOU ALWAYS DO?
WE'VE PREPARED A SPECIAL TYPE OF TEA FOR YOU TODAY.
IT'S A TEA MADE BY THAT GIRL USAGI OVER THERE.
AND WHO IS SHE?
WELL, THIS IS JUST BETWEEN US NOW...
...BUT SHE'S RANMARU MORI'S GIRLFRIEND.
PHOOT

## UE-RIN'S WAY OF THE MANGA 16

The reply from the editor came after 2-3 weeks, but after re-drawing (all the parts that were pointed out), I had to wait for the next response to come again. I couldn't bear all that waiting anymore, so I decided to send my manga to other publishers.

As for how that turned out... ...check out the next volume!

Send your messages and letters to the following address. We're looking forward to your requests for the Extra Missions as well!

Rinko Ueda
C/O Shojo Beat
Viz Media
P.O. Box 71010
San Francisco, CA
94107

Rinko Ueda

YOU SHOULD TRY SOME, RANMARU.
THE NOBLES SEEM TO LIKE YOUR TEA.

JU...
JUST GIVE IT A TRY...
I'LL HAVE SOME LATER.

SADA-NARI...
IT'S TOO EARLY TO START YAWNING.
HAAGH...
IT TASTES THE BEST WHEN IT'S FRESHLY BREWED...

IF YOU SAY SO...

I SUDDENLY FEEL SLEEPY...
SADA-NARI...
DRINK THIS WHILE IT'S STILL HOT...

WILL YOU FEED IT TO ME MOUTH TO MOUTH?
MOUTH...?
O...
GUSH
...OKAY!!
HUH?
USAGI...

MMMMM
WHA...
WHAT'S WRONG, SADANARI?!
THUD
ZZZ
SHATTER
ZZZ
NGH...

!!
CRASH
I...I FEEL SO... SLEEPY...
ZZZ
ZZZ
SWAY
SWAY
YOU TWO...
...NOT IN FRONT OF THE...
...GUESTS...
SHOVE
DID THE TEA...?!
DIZZY
WHAT DID YOU...
COME BACK HERE!!
DASH

SOMEBODY CAPTURE THAT GIRL!!
I HAVE TO GO BACK.
I HAVE TO GO BACK AND TELL HANZO...
TUG

YOU FOOL.
AHH
NOOO
BE QUIET!
SWAY
SWAY
ICHIJO NO KIMI...
...DON'T LET GO OF THAT GIRL...
FLUP
!!

YOU DON'T HAVE TO TELL ME NOT TO LET GO OF USAGI.
WHAT ARE YOU DOING...

HANZO...!!
TO BE CONTINUED...

***The ways of the ninja are mysterious indeed, so here is a glossary of terms to help you navigate the intricacies of their world.***

**Page 8, panel 4: Tokugawa Ieyasu**
Tokugawa Ieyasu (1543-1616) was the first Shogun of the Tokugawa Shogunate. He made a small fishing village named Edo the center of his activities. Edo thrived and became a huge town and was later renamed Tokyo, the present capital.

**Page 9, panel 4: Iga**
Iga is a region on the island of Honshu and also the name of the famous ninja clan that originated there. Another area famous for its ninja is Kouga, in the Shiga prefecture on Honshu. Many books claim that these two ninja clans were mortal enemies, but in reality inter-ninja relations were not as bad as stories might suggest.

**Page 15, panel 5: Manga School**
"Manga School" is a section in Japanese manga magazines for people who want to become manga artists. Participants who receive high scores for their sample manga submissions get an award along with a chance to make their debut in the magazine.

**Page 23, panel 3: Castella**
Castella is a type of sponge cake made from sugar, flour, eggs, and starch syrup. This sweet was brought over to Japan by Portuguese merchants and was originally called "pão de Castella" (meaning "bread from Castile").

**Page 32: Benkei**
Benkei is a character from Rinko Ueda's manga series *Ryo*. He is based on the Japanese historical figure Saito Musashibo Benkei, who is known for his strength and loyalty.

**Page 2: Shimo no Hanzo**
*Shimo no* means "the Lower," and in this case refers to Hanzo's geographic location rather than social status.

**Page 2: Azuchi**
Azuchi is by Lake Biwa in Shiga Prefecture, where Oda Nobunaga built his castle and the town that were the center of his operations.

**Page 2: Oda Nobunaga**
Nobunaga lived from 1534 to 1582, and came close to unifying Japan. He is probably one of the most famous Japanese warlords. He was the first warlord to successfully incorporate the gun in battle and is notorious for his ruthlessness.

**Page 2: Okazaki**
Okazaki is in Aichi Prefecture on the main island of Honshu, about 22 miles from Nagoya.

**Page 6: Matsuken Samba and Abarenbo Shogun**
The song "Matsuken Samba" was a big hit around 2005; it's sung by Japanese actor Ken Matsudaira ("Matsuken" is derived from combining the first syllable of his last name "Matsu" with his first name "Ken.") Ken Matsudaira is also famous for his role in a TV series called *Abarenbo Shogun*.

**Page 96, panel 1: Enryakuji**
Enryakuji is a famous temple on Mt. Hiei and was a significant symbol of Buddhism at the time. Because the Buddhists did not obey Nobunaga, he burned the temple to the ground in 1571, killing 20,000-30,000 men, women, and children in the process.

**Page 114, panel 3: Mitsuhide Akechi**
Mitsuhide Akechi became one of Oda Nobunaga's retainers after Nobunaga's conquest of Mino province (now Gifu prefecture) in 1566. Akechi is known to have been more of an intellectual and a pacifist than a warrior.

**Page 123, panel 4: Sakai**
Sakai is a city in Osaka prefecture that is one of the largest and most important seaports in Japan. Once known for samurai swords, Sakai is now famous for quality kitchen knives and other cutlery.

**Page 142, panel 2: Sen no Rikyu**
Sen no Rikyu (1522-1591) is famous for having a huge influence on the Japanese tea ceremony, particularly in wabi-cha (a style that emphasizes simplicity). Rikyu became tea master for Oda Nobunaga when he was 58 years old.

**Page 148, panel 6: Tempura**
Although tempura is now considered a classic Japanese dish, it was Portuguese missionaries who first introduced this batter-coated deep fried delicacy to Japan during the 16th century.

**Page 161: Kunoichi**
A term often used for female ninja. The word is spelled くノ一, and when combined, the letters form the kanji for woman, 女。

**Page 163: Plus Alpha**
In Japanese, "plus alpha" is used to amplify something. For example, if someone asks you how busy your work is, you might reply, "I'm pretty busy right now. I've got my usual stuff to do plus alpha on the side."

**Page 38, panel 3: Rubia Akane**
Rubia Akane is a plant that can be found in the mountains of Japan. Its root is used in Chinese and Japanese medicine to heal anemia, stop bleeding, etc. It is also used in cloth dyeing, as it has an orange yellow color when the root is dried.

**Page 58: Ryo**
Ryo is the title character of Rinko Ueda's manga series *Ryo*. The story features Saito Musashibo Benkei and Minamoto no Yoshitsune, two popular characters from Japanese history.

**Page 58: Juni-hitoe**
A juni-hitoe is a very elegant and complex kimono worn by court ladies in Japan. The name literally translates into "twelve-layer robe," and it can weigh up to 20 kilograms.

**Page 68, panel 2: Kami no Hanzou**
The term *kami no* means "the Upper," and can refer to social status. However, since Hanzou is a member of a branch family, it is very unlikely that his status is higher than that of the head of the entire clan, Hanzo. The term *kami no* can also refer to geographic location in relation to an important city center, such as the capital. Hanzou is from Okazaki, which is closer to Edo than Hanzo's home in Segachi.

**Page 77, panel 1: Ninjutsu**
Ninjutsu means the skill or ability of a ninja.

**Page 84: Guitar Samurai**
Guitar Samurai is a TV character played by Japanese comedian Yoku Hata. He appears in a man's kimono with a guitar and sings a song that usually makes fun of a famous celebrity. After imitating the celebrity, Guitar Samurai finishes by saying, "Slash!" Yoku Hata also uses the phrase "Isn't that what people say?" in his puns.

Usagi wasn't good at anything in the beginning, but lately she's been acting more like a kunoichi (which is something even I never expected to see). In addition, Hanzo seems to be becoming more human. I really enjoy showing these small changes. Usagi's encounter with Ranmaru has brought a big turning point in this story, so please continue to follow the adventures of Usagi and her friends.

–Rinko Ueda

Rinko Ueda is from Nara prefecture. She enjoys listening to the radio, drama CDs, and Rakugo comedy performances. Her works include *Ryo*, a series based on the legend of Gojo Bridge, *Home*, a story about love crossing national boundaries, and *Tail of the Moon (Tsuki no Shippo)*, a romantic ninja comedy.

# TAIL OF THE MOON

## Vol. 8

The Shojo Beat Manga Edition

STORY & ART BY
**RINKO UEDA**

Translation & Adaptation/Tetsuichiro Miyaki
Touch-up Art & Lettering/Mark McMurray
Design/Izumi Hirayama
Editor/Amy Yu

VP, Production/Alvin Lu
VP, Sales & Product Marketing/Gonzalo Ferreyra
VP, Creative/Linda Espinosa
Publisher/Hyoe Narita

TSUKI-NO SHIPPO © 2002 by Rinko Ueda. All rights reserved. First published in Japan in 2002 by SHUEISHA Inc., Tokyo. English translation rights arranged by SHUEISHA Inc.

The stories, characters and incidents mentioned in this publication are entirely fictional.

No portion of this book may be reproduced or transmitted in any form or by any means without written permission from the copyright holders.

The rights of the author(s) of the work(s) in this publication to be so identified have been asserted in accordance with the Copyright, Designs and Patents Act 1988. A CIP catalogue record for this book is available from the British Library.

Printed in Canada

Published by VIZ Media, LLC
P.O. Box 77064
San Francisco, CA 94107

Shojo Beat Manga Edition
10 9 8 7 6 5 4 3 2
First printing, December 2007
Second printing, September 2009

www.viz.com

store.viz.com

**PARENTAL ADVISORY**
TAIL OF THE MOON is rated T+ for Older Teen and is recommended for ages 16 and up. This volume contains brief nudity and ninja violence.
ratings.viz.com

# A Question of FATE

Tail of the Moon

Prequel: The Other Hanzo(u)

Story & Art by
Rinko Ueda

Found injured and unconscious in a bamboo field, a girl known only as Kaguya struggles to remember her identity. Little does she know that her fate is tied to Hanzou, a handsome castle bodyguard, and Hanzo, the leader of a ninja village. Will she ever realize her true destiny?

Find out in the *Tail of the Moon Prequel: The Other Hanzo(u)*—**IN STORES NOW!**

The story continues in *Tail of the Moon*, the wildly popular manga series featuring the ongoing story of Hanzo.

**ALL 15 VOLUMES NOW AVAILABLE!**

Shojo Beat
MANGA from the HEART

On sale at **www.shojobeat.com**
Also available at your local bookstore and comic store.

RATED T for OLDER TEEN
ratings.viz.com

viz media
www.viz.com

TSUKI-NO TOIKI AI-NO KIZU © 2001 by Rinko Ueda/SHUEISHA Inc.
TSUKI-NO SHIPPO © 2002 by Rinko Ueda/SHUEISHA Inc.

# Haruka
## -Beyond the Stream of Time-

By Tohko Mizuno

Akane is a typical teenage girl...until she swallows a Dragon Jewel and finds herself transported to ancient Japan! What will happen when she learns she's been foreordained to lead the people of Kyou as the Priestess of the Dragon God?

**Find out in the *Haruka: Beyond the Stream of Time* manga series!**

*On Sale Now*

On sale at:
**www.shojobeat.com**

Also available at your local bookstore and comic store.

Harukanaru Toki no Nakade © Tohko Mizuno, KOEI Co., Ltd. 1999/HAKUSENSHA, Inc.

www.viz.com

# LAND OF *Fantasy*

MIAKA YÛKI IS AN ORDINARY JUNIOR-HIGH STUDENT WHO IS SUDDENLY WHISKED AWAY INTO THE WORLD OF A BOOK, *THE UNIVERSE OF THE FOUR GODS*. WILL THE BEAUTIFUL CELESTIAL BEINGS SHE ENCOUNTERS AND THE CHANCE TO BECOME A PRIESTESS DIVERT MIAKA FROM EVER RETURNING HOME?

THREE VOLUMES OF THE ORIGINAL *FUSHIGI YÛGI* SERIES COMBINED INTO A LARGER FORMAT WITH AN EXCLUSIVE COVER DESIGN AND BONUS CONTENT

EXPERIENCE THE BEAUTY OF *FUSHIGI YÛGI* WITH THE HARDCOVER ART BOOK

ALSO AVAILABLE: THE *FUSHIGI YÛGI: GENBU KAIDEN* MANGA, THE EIGHT VOLUME PREQUEL TO THIS BEST-SELLING FANTASY SERIES

**On sale at www.shojobeat.com**

**Also available at your local bookstore and comic store.**

FUSHIGI YUGI © Yuu WATASE/Shogakukan Inc.
FUSHIGI YUGI GENBUKAIDEN © Yuu WATASE/Shogakukan Inc.
WATASE YUU IRASUTOSHU FUSHIGI YUGI © Yuu WATASE/Shogakukan Inc.

www.viz.com

TAKE A TRIP TO AN ANCIENT
FUSHIGI YÛGI
FROM THE CREATOR O
ABSOLUTE BOYFRIEND
ALICE 19TH, CERES:
CELESTIAL LEGEND,
AND IMADOKI!

# Black Bird

## BLOOD PROMISE

Otherworldly creatures have pursued Misao since childhood, and her onetime crush is the only one who can protect her. But at what cost?

**Find out in the *Black Bird* manga—buy yours today!**

**Winner of the 2009 Shogakukan Manga Award for Shojo**

**By Kanoko Sakurakoji**
**The creator of**
***Backstage Prince***

**www.shojobeat.com**
**Available at your local bookstore and comic store.**

Shojo Beat

RATED T FOR OLDER TEEN ratings.viz.com

VIZ media
www.viz.com

BLACK BIRD © Kanoko SAKURAKOUJI / Shogakukan Inc.

# We Were There

By Yuki Obata
Also known as the award-winning series *Bokura ga Ita*

## Get to the Bottom of a Broken Heart

It's love at first sight when Nanami Takahashi falls for Motoharu Yano, the most popular boy in her new class. But he's still grieving his girlfriend who died the year before. Can Nanami break through the wall that surrounds Motoharu's heart?

Find out in *We Were There*—
manga series on sale now!

www.viz.com

ratings.viz.com

On sale at www.shojobeat.com
Also available at your local
bookstore and comic store.

BOKURA GA ITA © Yuuki OBATA/Shogakukan Inc.

Story and Art by Miki Aihara | Creator of *Honey Hunt* and *Tokyo Boys & Girls*

Shojo Beat

**On sale at www.shojobeat.com**

**Also available at your local bookstore and comic store.**

HOT GIMMICK © Miki AIHARA/Shogakukan Inc.
HOT GIMMICK S © Miki AIHARA, Megumi NISHIZAKI/Shogakukan Inc.

RATED T FOR OLDER TEEN ratings.viz.com

viz media
www.viz.com

# Hot Gimmick

If you think being a teenager is hard, be glad your name isn't Hatsumi Narita

With scandals that would make any gossip girl blush and more triangles than you can throw a geometry book at, this girl may never figure out the game of love!

Tell us what you think about Shojo Beat Manga!
Our survey is now available online. Go to:
shojobeat.com/mangasurvey
Help us make our product offerings better!
viz media
Shojo Beat
MANGA from the HEART
THE REAL DRAMA BEGINS IN...
FULL MOON WO SAGASHITE © 2001 by Arina Tanemura/SHUEISHA Inc.
Fushigi Yûgi: Genbu Kaiden © 2004 Yuu WATASE/Shogakukan Inc.
Ouran Koko Host Club © Bisco Hatori 2002/HAKUSENSHA, Inc.